THE FAMOUS TEMPLES OF A REMARKABLE CIVILIZATION

Ancient Egypt History Books for 4th Grade

Children's Ancient History

In this book, we're going to talk about the temples of the Ancient Egyptians. So, let's get right to it!

Religion was at the core of the daily life of the Ancient Egyptians. They had many temples and, in most cases, the temple was constructed in honor of a specific god or goddess.

CATHOLICISM
ISLAM
BUDDHISM
ORTHODOXY
HINDUISM
JUDAISM

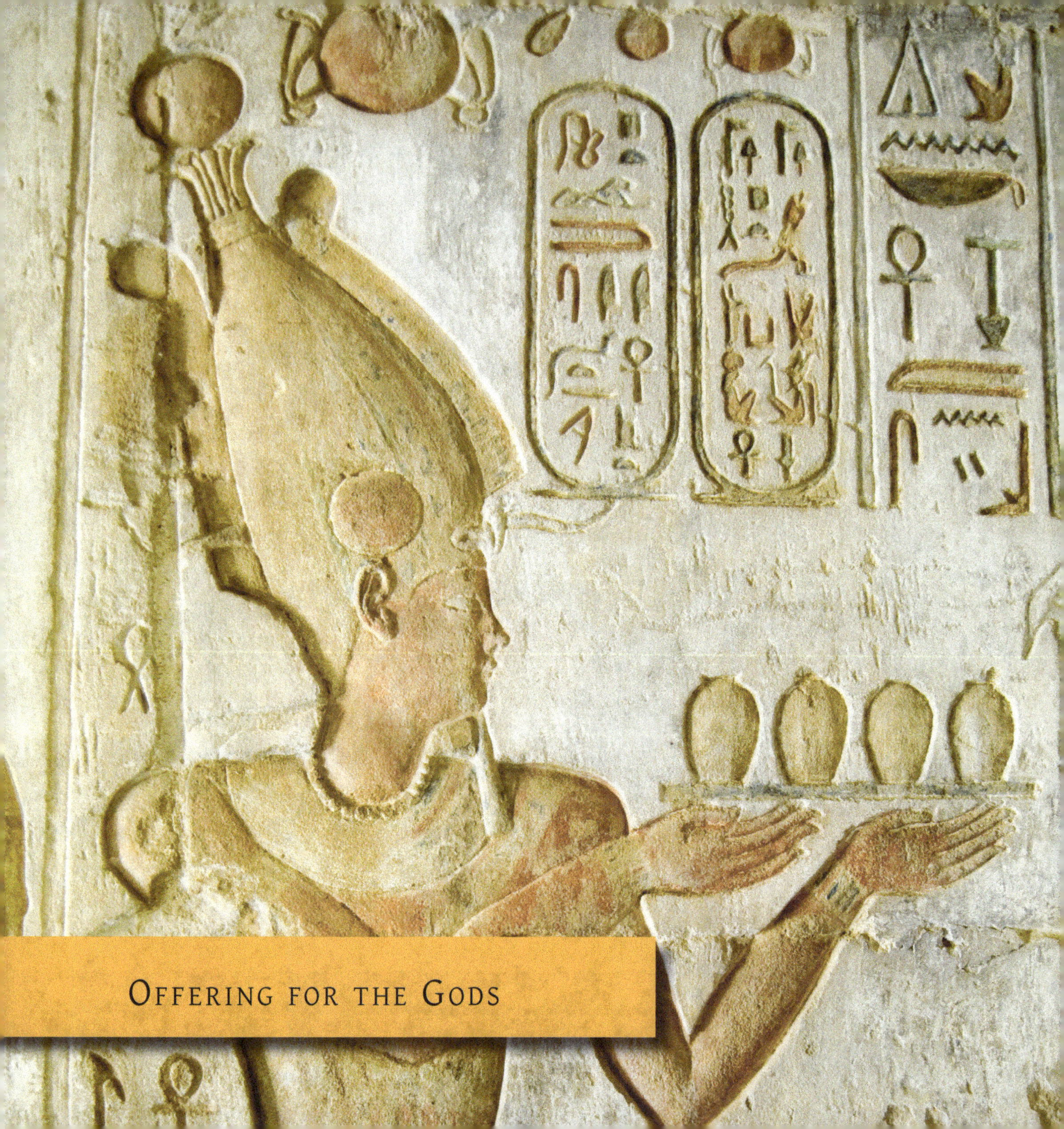
OFFERING FOR THE GODS

The Egyptians didn't worship in their temples. Instead, they brought offerings there to appease the gods. They also participated in festivals and rituals designed to show homage to their many gods. Most homes had small altars set aside where offerings to the gods could be placed.

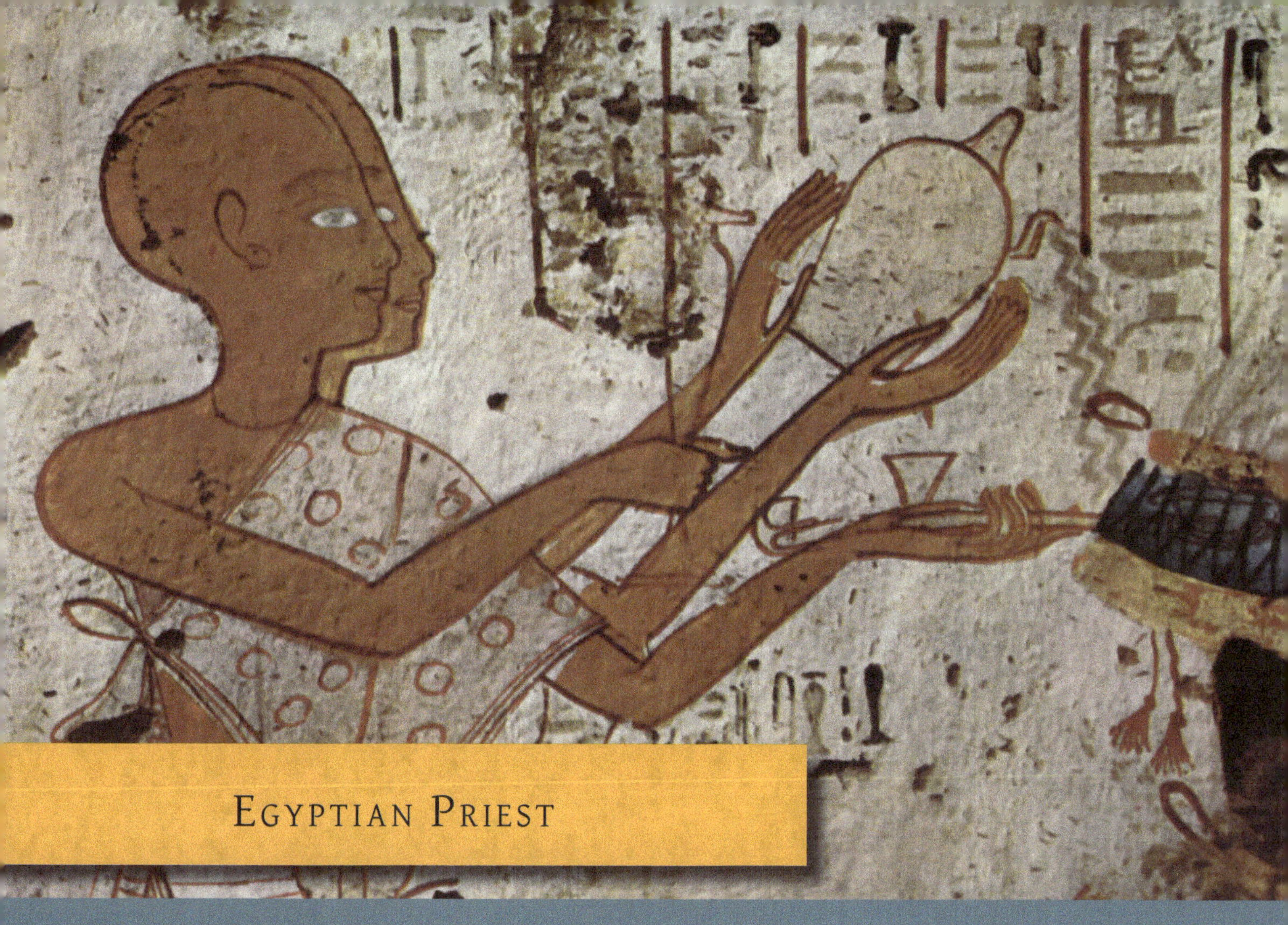

The temples and the priests associated with the temples had a lot of power in society. They were important for other reasons besides

the daily ritual practices. Many people were employed by the temples, including priests and craftsmen.

In order for them to feed the people they employed, the temples owned farmland. They received spoils from the Pharaoh's successful foreign battles. Sometimes the Pharaoh gave the temple a gift of additional land or goods to thank the gods for favors received.

ANCIENT EGYPTIAN FARMER

MORTUARY TEMPLE OF HATSHEPSUT

WHAT TYPES OF TEMPLES DID THE EGYPTIANS HAVE?

There were two types of temples in Ancient Egyptian civilizations. One type is called a cultus temple and the other is called a mortuary temple. A cultus or religious temple was really designed as a house or dwelling for a main god or goddess.

Other gods or goddesses may have been part of the temple as well, but there was always a main god or goddess. The priest would attend to the statues of the gods. He would perform ceremonies in the deity's honor and offer prayers and gifts. Some festivals or ceremonies were open so that other Egyptians could participate in the rituals.

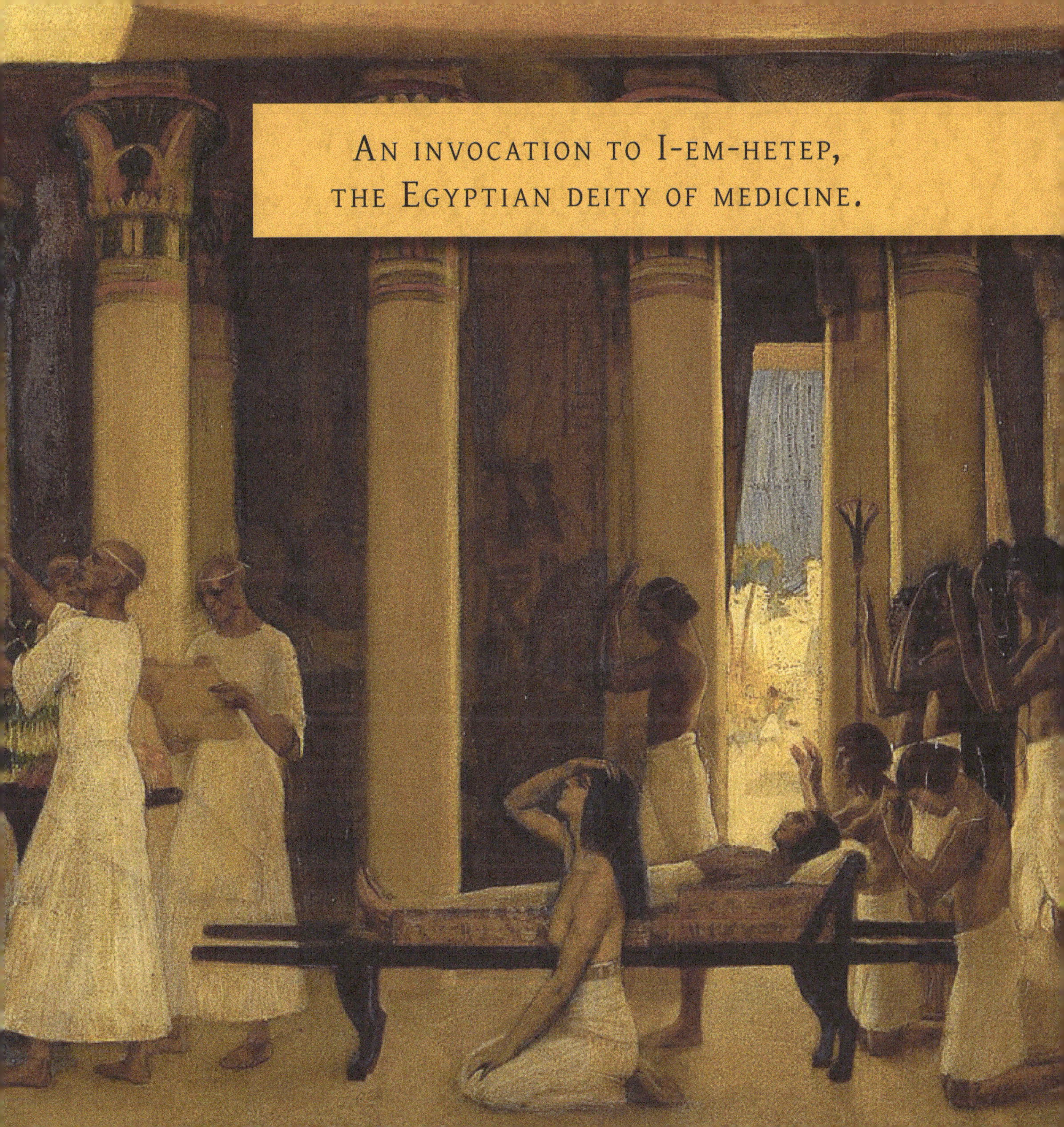
An invocation to I-em-hetep,
the Egyptian deity of medicine.

The other type of temple was a mortuary temple. The belief in an afterlife was at the center of the Egyptian's religious beliefs. As soon as a Pharaoh came into power, the planning for his or her departure for the afterlife began. The food, as well as the clothing and other items the Pharaoh would need, were attended to by a special group of people who were a funerary cult. These types of temples were only built for pharaohs.

Temple at Phile

At the beginning, the Egyptians built these mortuary temples as part of a complex that was devoted to the tomb. For example, many of the pyramids had mortuary temples built beside them. These were for the pharaohs who were buried in the tombs inside the pyramids.

SETI I TEMPLE

During the time that the pyramids were built, the Great Pyramid at Giza was designed as a tomb burial chamber for the Pharaoh Khufu. In that same complex, there was a mortuary temple

for Khufu as well. Later on, the pharaohs wanted their tombs to be hidden so that tomb raiders wouldn't break in, so they built the temples at a distance from their tombs.

FAMOUS EGYPTIAN TEMPLES

Many of the Egyptian temples were rebuilt in the same place over the centuries. The pharaohs documented what they did during the reconstruction periods. Many of the buildings are still partially standing as are their guardian statues.

RECONSTRUCTION OF ABUSIMBEL

TEMPLE OF KARNAK

KARNAK

Pharaoh Senusret I established the Temple at Karnak in 3200 BC. It is the largest of the temple complexes in Egypt and ranks second largest for ancient temple complexes after Cambodia's Angkor Wat. There was construction on the temple during the entire time of Ancient Egypt, over 3,000 years and during the reigns of thirty different Pharaohs. This makes the architecture of the Karnak complex quite diverse.

The city of Thebes where Karnak is located was a religious hub. This location in the southern part of Egypt is now called the city of Luxor. The temple was designed as the dwelling of the "god of gods," Amun, with his son called Khonsu, and his wife named Mut. It had four different temple complexes in separate precincts. The temple priests built chapels dedicated to other deities in each of the precincts and each had a sacred pool area.

COLUMNS OF THE TEMPLE OF KARNAK

HYPOSTYLE HALL

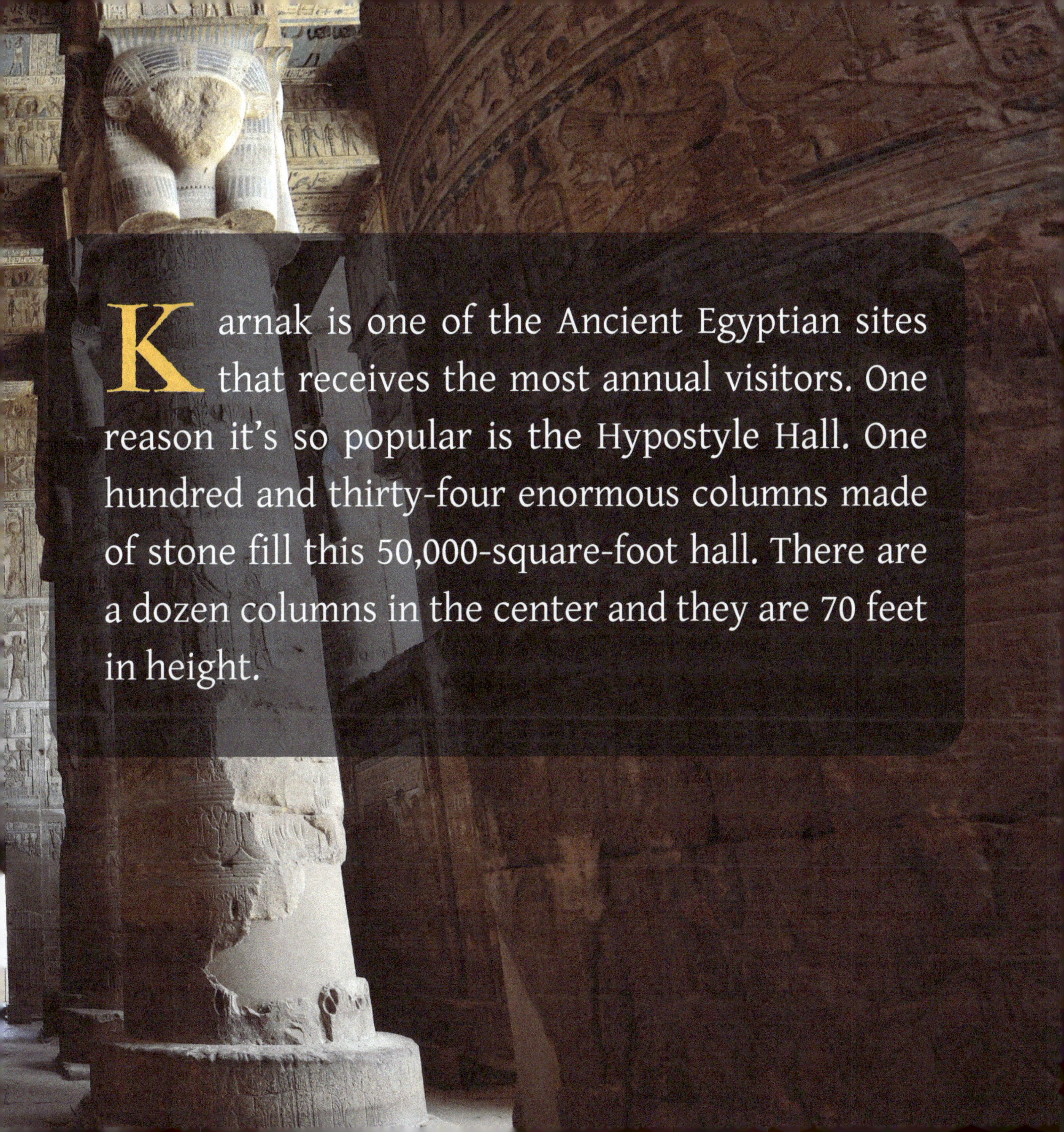

K arnak is one of the Ancient Egyptian sites that receives the most annual visitors. One reason it's so popular is the Hypostyle Hall. One hundred and thirty-four enormous columns made of stone fill this 50,000-square-foot hall. There are a dozen columns in the center and they are 70 feet in height.

LUXOR TEMPLE

The Luxor Temple is located south of Karnak on the Nile River's east bank. Constructed around 1400 BC, the temple was designed as a dwelling for the Theban Triad of gods, Amun, his wife, and his son. The Opet religious festival took place there every year. During this time, the Amun statue would be moved in a ceremony from the Temple at Karnak to the Temple at Luxor.

LUXOR TEMPLE

he Temple at Luxor is also known for its immense statues of Ramesses II. Another famous location there is the Avenue of the Sphinx. Also notable is an obelisk made of red granite that is 80 feet in height. There used to be a second obelisk, but one of them was moved to Paris.

ABU SIMBEL

Located on Egypt's southern border, the two Abu Simbel temples are marvels of engineering. Ramesses II built them between 1264 to 1244 BC. They were constructed as a shrine to himself and also Queen Nefertari, his principal wife.

Abu Simbel Temple Egypt Pharaohs

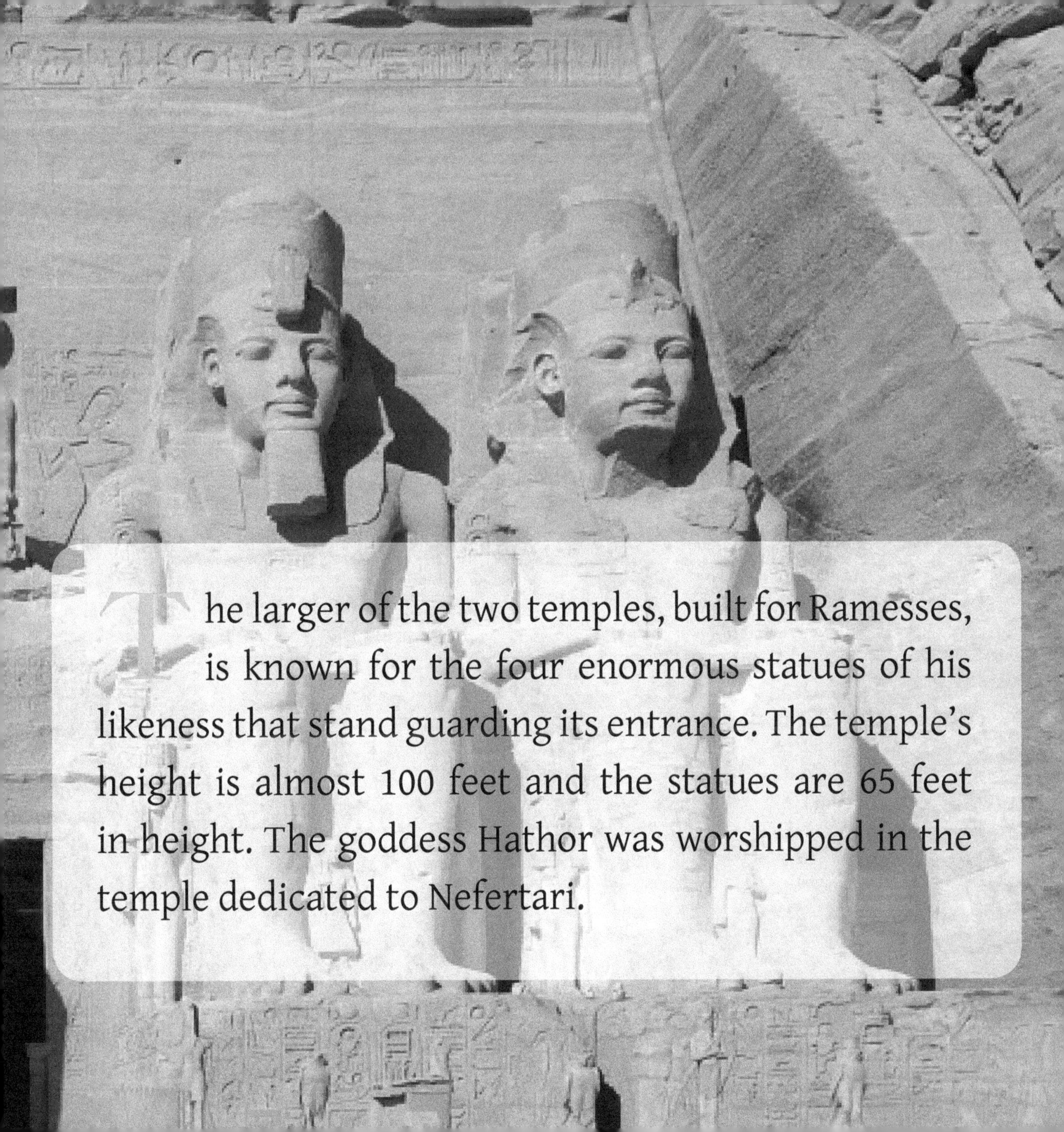

The larger of the two temples, built for Ramesses, is known for the four enormous statues of his likeness that stand guarding its entrance. The temple's height is almost 100 feet and the statues are 65 feet in height. The goddess Hathor was worshipped in the temple dedicated to Nefertari.

These amazing temples showed Ramesses' power to his neighbors to the south. The Egyptians carved these temples from the mountain and they were in danger of flooding from the Aswan Dam, so Egyptologists moved them in 1968.

TEMPLE OF EDFU

THE TEMPLE AT EDFU

Located at the Nile River's west bank, this temple was built from 237 BC to 57 BC, during the reign of the Ptolemaic Dynasty. It was constructed over a temple that had been built during the New Kingdom.

A few pyramids have been found near the site and Egyptologists are researching them to uncover their original builders. The god Horus, the sky god with the head of a falcon, was worshipped there.

STATUE OF HORUS

Hatshepsut's Mortuary Temple

HATSHEPSUT'S MORTUARY TEMPLE

Located northeast of the modern city of Luxor, close to the Valley of the Kings, is the mortuary temple designed to house the body of Hatshepsut, one of Egypt's female pharaohs. It was built in 1470 BC and represented a departure from the typical temple architecture of that time period.

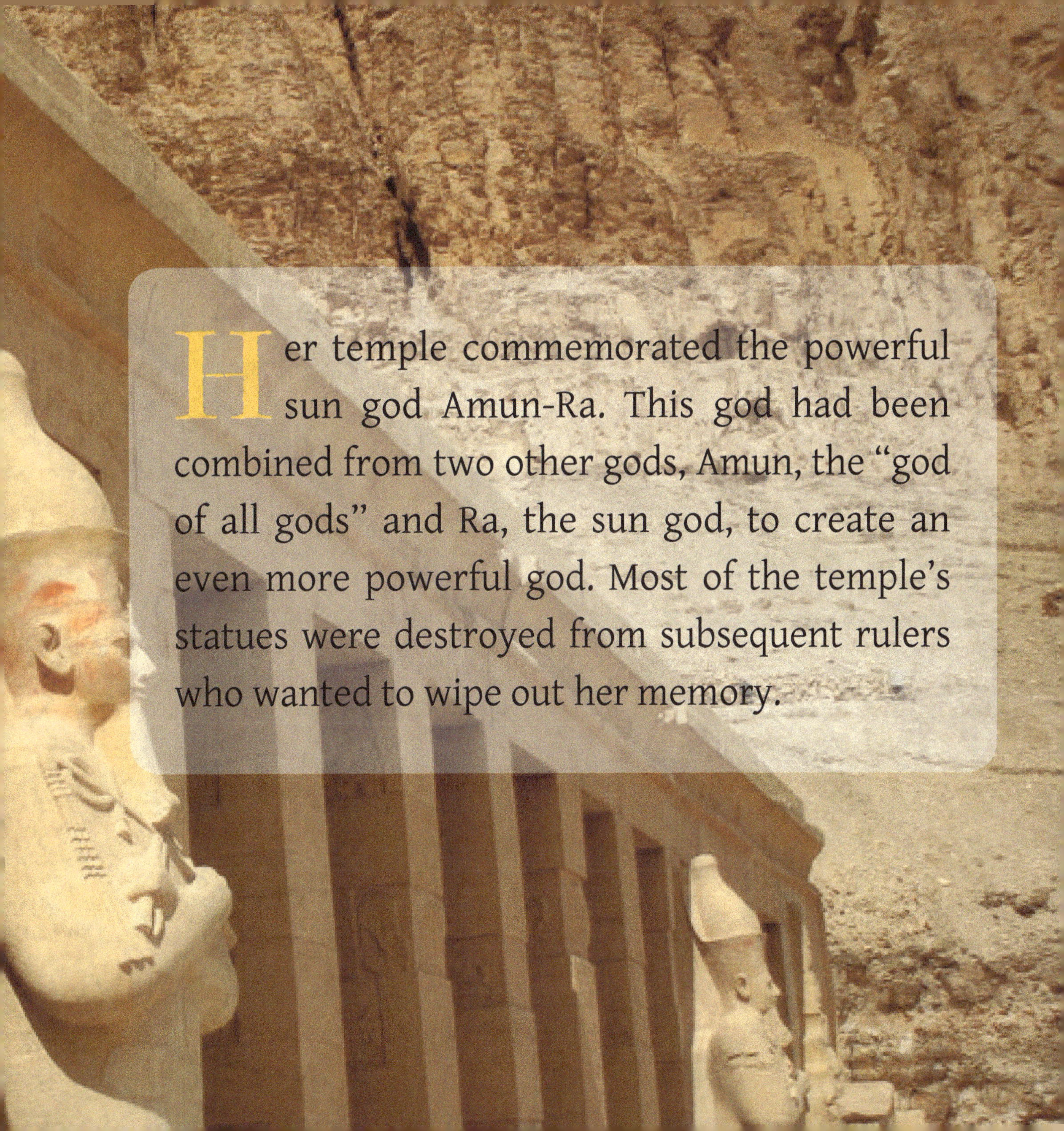

er temple commemorated the powerful sun god Amun-Ra. This god had been combined from two other gods, Amun, the "god of all gods" and Ra, the sun god, to create an even more powerful god. Most of the temple's statues were destroyed from subsequent rulers who wanted to wipe out her memory.

Temple of philae

THE TEMPLES OF PHILAE

These temples were constructed on an island in the middle of the Nile River. Over a long period of time, the temples were built by pharaohs, and then temples built by the Greeks and Romans were built at the same site. The main Egyptian temple was designed for the goddess Isis. She was the goddess of fertility and motherhood.

KOM OMBO

This temple has a unique double structure. There were two sets of everything along a center axis—two courts, two halls, and two sanctuaries. It was built during the Ptolemaic reign about 180 BC to 47 BC.

TEMPLE OF KOM OMBO

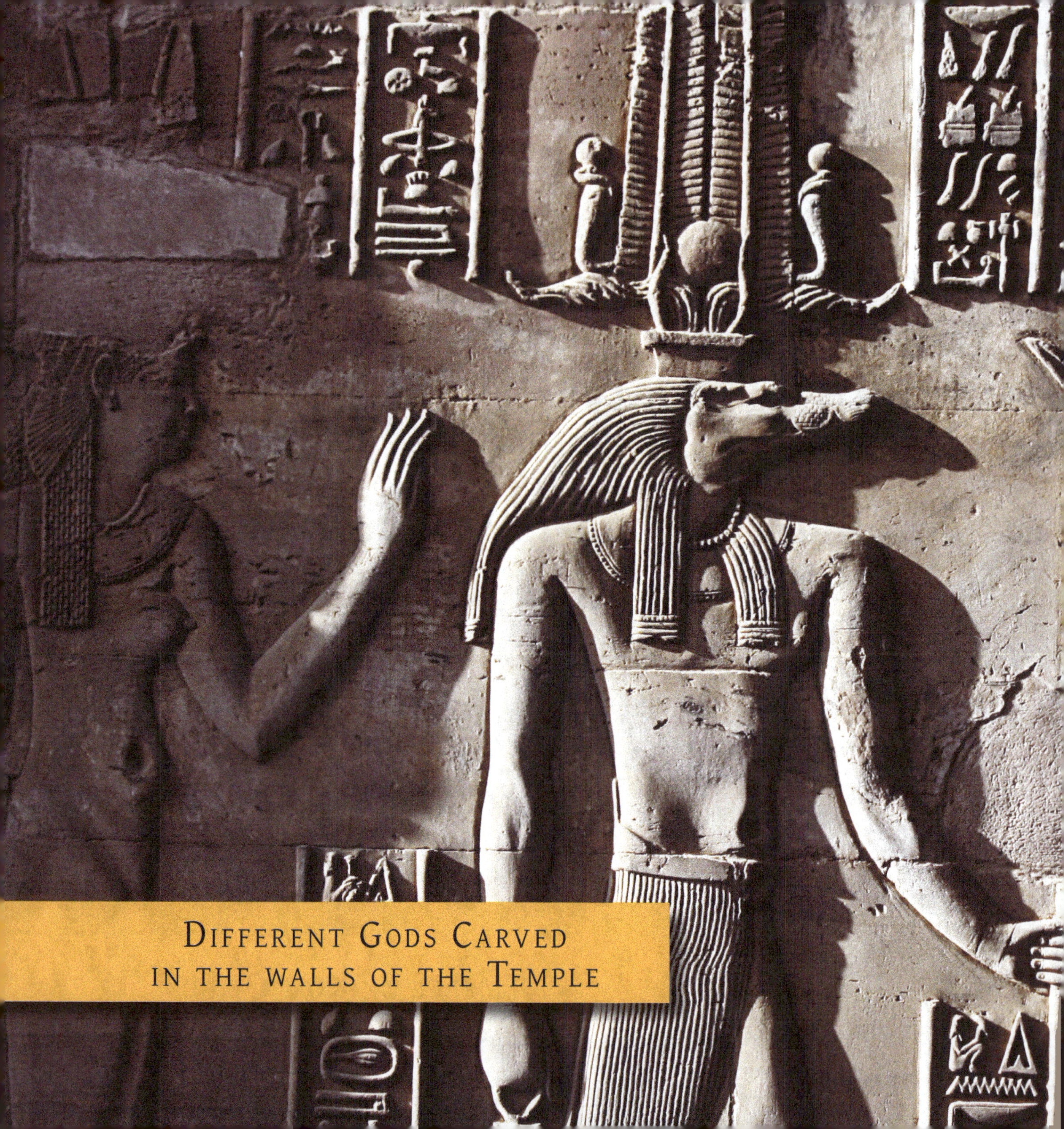

DIFFERENT GODS CARVED
IN THE WALLS OF THE TEMPLE

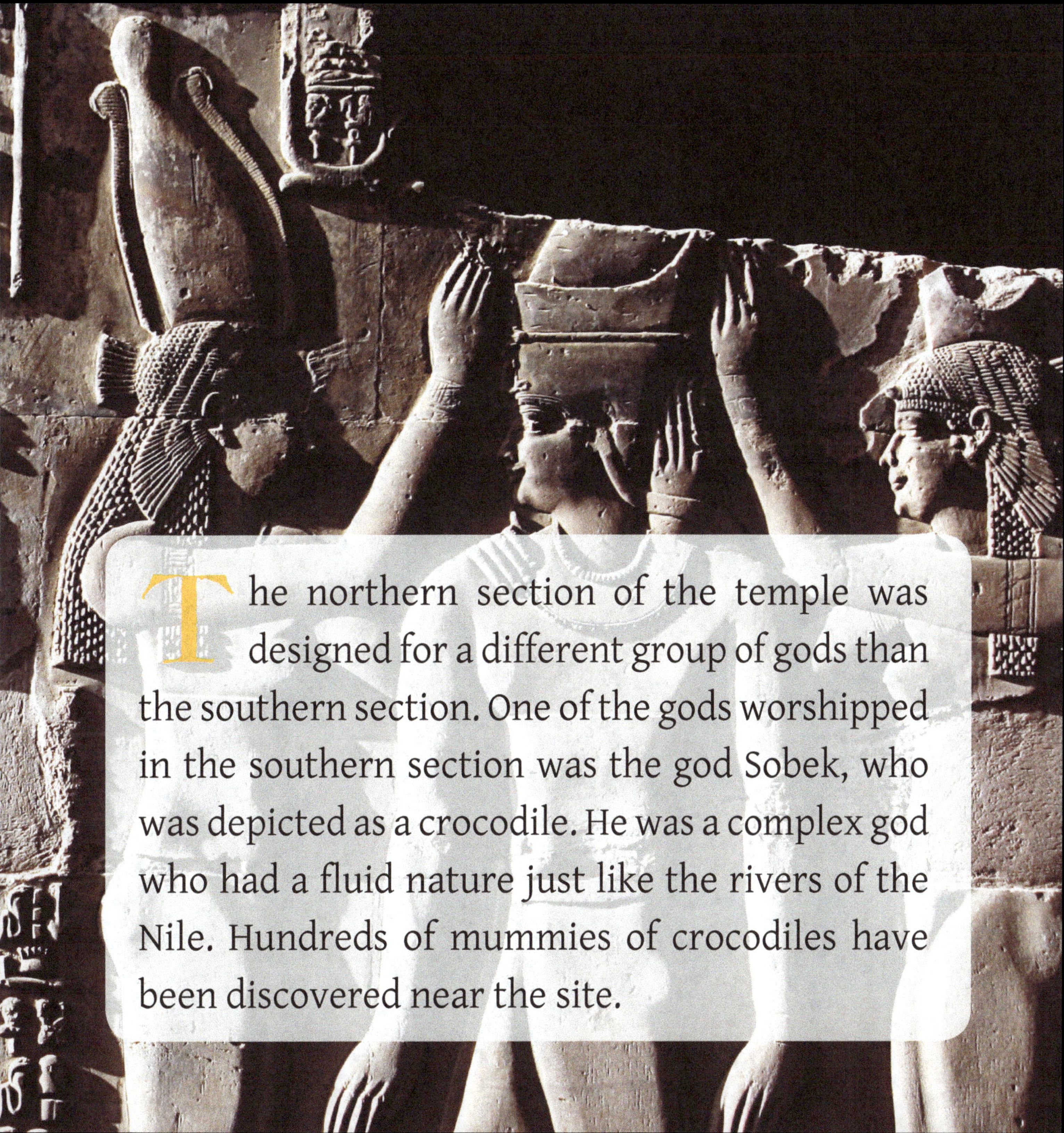

The northern section of the temple was designed for a different group of gods than the southern section. One of the gods worshipped in the southern section was the god Sobek, who was depicted as a crocodile. He was a complex god who had a fluid nature just like the rivers of the Nile. Hundreds of mummies of crocodiles have been discovered near the site.

THE TEMPLE OF SETI I

This mortuary temple was built around 1280 BC and designed for Seti I. Located in the modern-day city of Abydos, it's designed in the shape of an "L." It has shrines dedicated to six different gods:

SETI I TEMPLE

SHRINE OF SETIS

- Osiris, the god of the underworld and the afterlife

- Isis, the goddess of fertility

- Horus, the sky god, who was the son of Osiris and Isis

- Amun, the main god or "king of the gods"

- Ra-Horakhty, god of the rising sun

- Ptah, god of craftsmen and architects

There was also a shrine dedicated to Seti I since he had been made into a god.

DENDERA

This complex is enormous and covers an area over 40,000 square meters. It is a very well preserved site with numerous buildings from different periods of Egyptian history. The main temple is dedicated to the goddess of love named Hathor. Egyptologists have found many notable artifacts there including a relief sculpture depicting the Dendera light, which some people believe may have been a type of electrical light, and the Dendera zodiac.

Dendera Temple

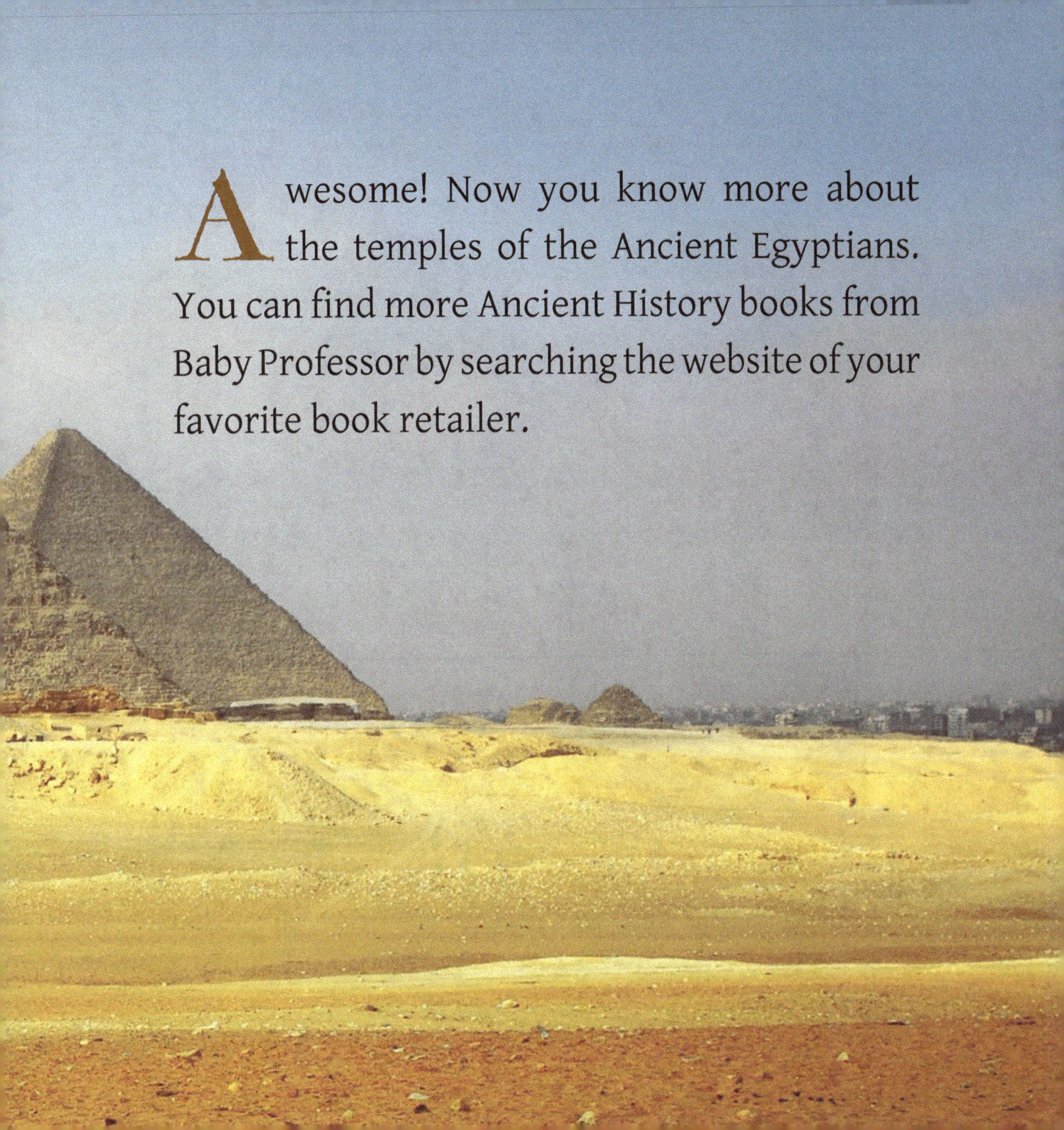

Awesome! Now you know more about the temples of the Ancient Egyptians. You can find more Ancient History books from Baby Professor by searching the website of your favorite book retailer.

Visit
BABY PROFESSOR
EDUCATION KIDS
www.BabyProfessorBooks.com
to download Free Baby Professor eBooks
and view our catalog of new and exciting
Children's Books